CONTENT

1. APPLE SALAD AND CHICKPEAS
2. BAMI
3. BANANA FRITTERS
4. BANANA NA BINYA
5. BITTERBALLEN
6. BOLO PRETU
7. BREAD PUDDING
8. CABBAGE & RAISINS
9. CARROT AND POTATO MASH
10. CASHEW CAKE
11. COCONUT TARTS
12. CORN BREAD
13. FRIKANDEL
14. FUNCHI
15. HANGOP
16. JOHNNY CAKES
17. KESIO
18. KRENTENBROOD
19. KROKETTEN
20. OLIE BOLLEN
21. PASTECHIS
22. PEAS SOUP
23. PICA
24. PINDA SAUCE
25. PRUNE CUPS
26. RYSTEBRY
27. SATE
28. STOBA
29. STOOFPEREN
30. STUFFING

APPLE SALAD AND CHICKPEAS

2 cans of chickpeas*
2 large red apples
2 ounces apple juice
3 ounces raisins
1 ounce butter
2-3 pounds chicken (diced)
1 large onion
Black pepper
5 tablespoons cooking oil (for frying)

For the Apple Salad
In a medium bowl: Peel, core, and roughly chop the apples. Mix in the apple juice and raisins. Allow to marinate. This is the apple salad.

For the Chickpeas
In a second medium bowl: Drain the chickpeas and rinse with cold water.

In a large frying pan: Heat the butter and fry the diced chicken to almost crispy. Add onion and fry for 1 minute more. Add the chickpeas, and allow to heat through for about 3 minutes; season with pepper to your taste.
Serve with the apple salad as a side.

*One large can and one small can

BAMI

½ cabbage (white)
10 sausages*
4 eggs
1 teaspoon salt
4 cloves of garlic (minced)
1 onion (minced)
2 cups spaghetti (pre-cooked)
1 red pepper
1 tablespoon black pepper
3 tablespoons soy sauce**
4 tablespoons cooking oil (for frying)

In a medium sauce pan: Slice the cabbage into medium pieces and cook until medium-tender about 10 minutes. Set aside.

Boil the sausages for about 10 minutes, then cut them into pieces and set aside.

In a small frying pan: Fry and scramble the eggs with a teaspoon of salt.

In a wok: Add garlic and onion. Add sausages, spaghetti, cabbage, red and black pepper, scrambled eggs, and soy sauce. Mix well and fry on high heat for about 3 minutes stirring frequently.

*Can use beef, chicken, or turkey sausage

**Traditional Ketjap Manis is available at Dutchsweets.com

BANANA FRITTERS

2 cups mashed bananas*
1 egg
1 tablespoon almond essence
¼ cup brown sugar
1 tablespoon cinnamon
1 cup milk
1 tablespoon olive oil
1 cup raisins
1 teaspoon salt
¾ cup all-purpose flour
1 teaspoon baking powder
Cooking oil (for frying)

Powdered sugar and/or sliced bananas (for garnish)

In a medium bowl: Mix together mashed bananas and egg. Add almond essence, sugar, cinnamon, milk, olive oil, raisins, and salt. Mix well. Slowly add in flour and baking powder, mixing until smooth.

In a large frying pan: Lightly cover the bottom of the pan in oil and heat before adding, pancake-sized, scoops of the batter; fry until golden brown on both sides. The cooking oil should not completely cover the fritters.

Drain on paper towels before serving.

Optional: Sprinkle with powdered sugar, or garnish with sliced bananas.

*Pumpkin can be substituted for the bananas (simply use 2 cups of boiled and mashed pumpkin).

BANANA NA BINYA
(Plantains-in-wine)

4 plantains (ripe)
½ cup brown sugar
3 teaspoons cinnamon
1½ cups sherry wine
1 cup olive oil (for frying)

Peel and cut the plantains in halves, then slice each half lengthwise.

In a large frying pan: Heat olive oil before adding plantains; fry until medium brown on each side.

In a large baking dish: Place fried slices separately, side by side, in the dish. Mix together sugar, cinnamon and wine. Pour the mixture over the plantains. (Plantains should be covered with wine.) Preheat oven to 350º and bake for 30 minutes. The finished dish should be reddish in color.

Serve warm.

BITTERBALLEN
(Round croquettes)

For the Filling
3 tablespoon butter
4 tablespoons flour {dual usage}
¾ cup beef stock
1½ Cups cooked ground meat*
1 tablespoon parsley
1 tablespoon black pepper

For the Crust
2 packets cracker crumbs (finely crushed)
2 eggs beaten
8 tablespoons water
3 cups cooking oil (for frying)

To Prepare the Filling
In a large skillet: Add butter, flour {3 tablespoons} and stock over medium heat. Stir into a thick sauce or paste. Then add ground meat, parsley, salt, and pepper. Mix together. Allow to cool, and refrigerate for about 45 minutes. With your hands: Shape the cooled meat mixture into balls (meatball size).

To Prepare the Crust
In three bowls: Bowl 1: add the cracker crumbs.
Bowl 2: add lightly beaten eggs.
Bowl 3: add water. Roll the meatballs in the first bowl and completely cover the meatballs with cracker crumbs. Then dip the cracker-covered meatballs in the eggs, followed by the water and, once again, the cracker crumbs. Be sure they are covered very well to create a "solid crust."

To Cook the Bitterballen
In a deep fryer: Fry the Bitterballen until deep brown (or a rich golden brown), for about 3-5 minutes.

Drain on paper towels.

Serve by spearing with toothpicks and using a side of spicy mustard as a dip.

*Cooked veal, ham, chicken, or shrimp.

BOLO PRETU
(Black cake)

½ pound dried fruit (mixed)
1 pound prunes
1 pound currants
1 pound raisins
1 pound dates
½ pound figs
2 cups cherry cordial {dual usage}
1 cup Cognac
1 cup red wine
½ pound butter

3 teaspoons almond essence
1 cup molasses
1 teaspoon cinnamon
6 eggs
2½ cups flour
1½ teaspoons baking powder
6 tablespoons black food coloring
Crisco or butter (to grease the baking pan)
1 pound brown sugar

In a large bowl: Blend together(food processor) until smooth, on low speed, the dried fruits, prunes, currants, raisins, dates, figs, cherry cordial{1 cup},Cognac, and red wine. Pour into an airtight container, cover and refrigerate for a minimum of 7 days.
In a medium bowl: Blend butter and the sugar until soft and creamy. Add almond essence, molasses, and cinnamon. Continue to blend for about 2 more minutes

In a second medium bowl: Beat the eggs very well.
In a clean large bowl: Mix together eggs and creamed butter and sugar. Add the fruit mix from the refrigerator. Blend for about 10 minutes. Slowly blend in flour and baking powder, followed by food coloring.

In large baking pan(s): Grease the pan(s). Preheat the oven to 300º. Pour the batter into the pan(s) and bake for about 1½ hours, rotating frequently in intervals of about 20 minutes. A toothpick inserted near the center of the cake should come out clean when the cake is fully baked.

Allow to cool completely. Slowly pour the last of cherry cordial {1 cup} over the entire cake. The cake will be moist.
Wrap the entire cake in foil and refrigerate until ready to serve.

BREAD PUDDING

2 cups milk
¾ cup brown sugar
3 tablespoons butter
1 teaspoon salt
3 tablespoons cinnamon
2 eggs
2 tablespoons anise
15 slices brown bread
1 cup water
½ cup raisins
Butter (to grease baking dish)
Cinnamon and anise (to coat baking dish)
Powdered sugar (for garnish)

In a large bowl: Combine milk, sugar, butter, salt, cinnamon, eggs, and anise, blend on low for about 6-10 minutes.

In a medium bowl: Soak the bread in water. Use a fork to mash it into small pieces and add to the large bowl and mix in raisins.

In a medium baking dish: Grease well. Cover the greased surface with anise and cinnamon, and then pour in the batter. Bake at 350º for 60 minutes uncovered for the first 30 minutes, then covered with aluminum foil for the final 30 minutes.
Cool.
Sprinkle with powdered sugar and serve

CABBAGE AND RAISINS

¼ cup butter
1 onion (minced)
2 apples (minced)
1 red cabbage (sliced)
1½ cups orange juice
2 tablespoons brown sugar
1 tablespoon cinnamon
2 whole garlic cloves
2 bay leaves
½ cup raisins
Optional - 1 tablespoon powdered ginger

In a large sauce pan: Add butter, onion and apples. Cook for about 3 minutes, over low heat, until soft. Add the cabbage, orange juice, sugar, cinnamon, cloves, bay leaves, and raisins. (Optional: Add ginger.) Cover and braise over low heat for 20 minutes until cooked through, stirring occasionally.

Before serving, remove the cloves and bay leaves.

Serve warm.

CARROT AND POTATO MASH

5 cups water {dual usage}
8 ounces beef stew
2 tablespoons of ground black pepper {dual usage}
4 tablespoons butter {dual usage}
3 onions (sliced)
4 tablespoons of parsley
4 boiled potatoes (cut into chunks)
½ cup shredded carrots
1 tablespoon of anise

In a large sauce pan: Bring water {3½ cups} to boil, add meat and black pepper {1 tablespoon}, lower heat and continue to cook for about 40 minutes.

In a large (deep) frying pan: Fry the meat in butter {3 tablespoons} for about 5 minutes. Add onions, water {1 cup}, parsley, and pepper {1 tablespoon}.Cover and simmer for 30-40 minutes over medium heat.

In a medium sauce pan: Add potatoes, carrots, anise, and water {½ cup}. Cover the pan and steam for about 10 minutes over high heat. Mash the potatoes and carrots with butter {1 tablespoon}.

Combine the meat and potatoes and blend together until smooth.

Serve warm.

CASHEW CAKE

For the Cake
1 cup margarine
1 cup sugar
6 egg whites
¼ teaspoon salt
1½ teaspoons baking powder
2 tablespoons almond essence
1 cup milk
2 cups cashews (ground)
1½ cups flour

For the Icing
3 egg whites
1 cup confectioner's sugar
$1/3$ cup margarine
1 teaspoon salt
2 teaspoons almond essence
1 cup ground cashews
½ cup chopped cherries

To Prepare the Cake
In a large bowl: Blend margarine and sugar together until completely smooth, mix in egg whites, salt, baking powder, almond essence, milk, and cashews. Blend for about 5 minutes. Finally, add in flour and mix the batter for about 5-10 minutes. Pour batter into a large well-greased cake pan and bake at 350º for 45 minutes to 1hour.(A toothpick inserted near the center of the cake should come out clean).

To Prepare the Icing
Allow the cake to completely cool.
In a large bowl: Blend egg whites with sugar. Add margarine, salt, and almond essence and blend until smooth. Finally mix in cashews.

To Assemble the Cake
Slice the cake in half (horizontally) and cover the center of the cake with icing. Replace the top half of the cake and cover the entire cake with icing. Garnish the top of the cake with cherries.

COCONUT TARTS

4 eggs (beaten)
½ cup sugar
½ cup butter (melted)
1 tablespoon lemon juice
1 teaspoon olive oil
2 teaspoons almond*
2 cups coconut water
1¼ cups grated coconut (or flakes)
8-12 pre-made pie/tart shells/cups*
Optional - cherries (minced)

In a large sauce pan: Blend together eggs, sugar, butter, lemon juice, oil, almond essence and coconut water until smooth (about 2 minutes). Stir in the coconut flakes. Cook on medium heat for 20 minutes. Cool for 30 minutes then pour into tart shells.

Refrigerate until ready to serve. Garnish with cherries for added flavor and décor.

*You could also use vanilla or sweet rum.

**This would also fill one 9" pre-baked pie/tart crust.

CORN BREAD

3 cups water
½ teaspoon salt
2 eggs
½ cup powdered milk
2½ cups sugar
1½ cups baking powder
3½ cups cornmeal
2 cups flour

In a large bowl: Blend together water, salt, eggs, powdered milk, sugar, and baking powder at low speed for 10 minutes. The batter should be very smooth. Add cornmeal and flour, continuing to blend for 10 more minutes.

In a medium to large baking pan: Heat oven to 350º degrees and bake the batter until golden brown (about 30 minutes). When the corn bread is ready, a toothpick inserted near the center of the bread should come out clean.

Serve warm

FUNCHI
(Corn meal mush)

1½ cups water (cold)
1 cup corn meal
1 teaspoon salt
1 tablespoon sugar
½ cup milk (hot)
1 tablespoon butter
Butter (for greasing the bowls)

In a medium sauce pan: Stir together water, corn meal, salt and sugar over medium heat for about 4 minutes. Slowly add hot milk and butter and continue to stir.

Bring to a boil over high heat. Reduce heat to medium low and cook, all the while stirring, until the mixture thickens and no longer sticks to the sides of the pan. (It should not harden.)

In a deep bowl (soup bowl size): Grease the bowl with butter. Heap a large spoonful (¼ cup) of the corn meal mixture into the bowl .Cover the bowl with a plate and swirl around to form the corn meal mixture into a "ball." You can create "smaller balls" per serving.

Serve with your favorite fish dish.

FRIKANDEL
(Dutch sausage)

½ cup onion (minced)
2 potatoes (mashed)
2 eggs (beaten)
1 garlic clove (minced)
1 pound ground beef
1 pound chicken (minced)
1½ teaspoons black pepper
1 teaspoon nutmeg
1 teaspoon of ground allspice
2-3 cups water (for boiling)
2 cups cooking oil (for frying)

In a large bowl: Mix together onion, mashed potato, eggs, garlic and ground beef and chicken. Add pepper, nutmeg and allspice. Roll into "sausage rolls."

In a large saucepan: Bring water to a boil. Add Frikandel and boil over high heat for 10 minutes.

In a deep-fryer: Fry Frikandel for 3 minutes on high heat.

Drain on paper towels.

You can make a "Frikandel Speciaal" as follows: Cut the Frikandel through the middle, lengthwise and add Pica (Hot Onions, recipe is above), mayonnaise, and Hela curry ketchup*.

*HELA curry ketchup is available at Amazon.com

HANGOP
(Prune curd)

1 cup red wine
Juice of 1 orange
½ teaspoon orange rind
1 tablespoon brown sugar
½ teaspoon nutmeg
½ cup water
1 cup prunes
4 cups plain yoghurt (for serving)

In a medium saucepan: Mix together wine, orange juice, orange rind, sugar, and nutmeg. Bring to a boil. Add water and prunes and simmer over low heat for about 15-20 minutes, until the prunes are covered in a "syrup-like" sauce. Allow to cool.

Serve in four soup bowls. Add the yoghurt first, and then spoon the prunes with sauce over the yoghurt.

JOHNNY CAKES
(Fried bread)

4 cups flour
2 teaspoons baking powder
1 tablespoon sugar
1 teaspoon salt
2 tablespoons butter
1 cup water
$1/3$ cup milk
2 cups cooking oil (for frying)

In a large bowl: Mix together flour, baking powder, sugar, and salt. Blend in butter. Mix in water and milk until smooth. Knead the dough into one big ball, cover with a cloth and let it stand for 15 -20minutes. Cut and roll the dough into golf-ball-sized pieces, then flatten them out into flat cakes.

In a deep fryer: Heat oil to a medium heat before adding dough and cook until medium brown.

Drain excess oil on paper towels.

Serve warm with any bread spread, but try Gouda cheese for a real treat.

KESIO

4 eggs
¼ teaspoon of salt
7 tablespoons sugar {dual usage}
1¼ cups condensed milk
1½ cups evaporated milk
1½ teaspoons vanilla

In a large bowl: Beat eggs with salt. Gradually add sugar {4 tablespoons}, beating until the sugar is dissolved. Stir in condensed milk and evaporated milk with vanilla.

In the top of a double boiler: On low heat, add sugar {3 tablespoons}, stirring constantly with a wooden spoon, until the sugar becomes caramel syrup. Remove from the stove and allow it to cool.

Pour the mixture from the large bowl into the double boiler with the caramelized sugar. Place over simmering water for about 35-50 minutes. Heat any hardened mixture, stuck to the boiler's sides, until it melts.

Cool the Kesio in the double boiler before serving

KRENTENBROOD
(Currant bread)

1¾ cups flour
1 teaspoon salt
3 tablespoons brown sugar {dual usage}
1½ cups currants
1 cup milk (warm) {dual usage}
1 ounce yeast
2½ tablespoons butter
1 egg
Butter (for greasing the pan)
Water (for basting)

In a large bowl: Add flour, salt, and sugar {2 tablespoons} and mix together.
In a medium bowl: Add milk {½ cup}, yeast, and the rest of the sugar {1 tablespoon}. Mix gently while it bubbles and dissolves.

In a medium cup: Melt butter with the remainder of the warm milk {½ cup}.
Pour the medium bowl's contents into the large bowl. Add the currants, egg and the butter/milk mixture. Mix well until it is smooth and without lumps.

Knead the dough (about 10 minutes), until the dough is very smooth, then form it into a ball. Cover with a damp towel and allow it to rise (almost double its size) for about 45 minutes.

In a loaf pan: Pour the batter into a well-greased pan and bake at 395º for 30 minutes until golden brown. (A toothpick inserted near the center of the bread should come out clean).

Remove the loaf from the oven and brush the top with water and bake for another minute.

Serve with your favorite spread. It is absolutely delicious with Gouda cheese.

KROKETTEN

For the Filling
1 onion minced
2 tablespoons parsley
5 tablespoons butter
1½ cups beef stock
½ cup white wine
½ cup flour
2 pounds ground beef (cooked)*

For the Crust
¼ cup flour
3 eggs
4 cups breadcrumbs
3 cups cooking oil (for frying)
¼ teaspoon salt
¼ teaspoon nutmeg
¼ teaspoon pepper

To Prepare the Filling
In a large skillet: Sauté the onion. Add parsley, butter, stock, wine, and flour. Mix into a paste or thick sauce. Add meat, pepper, salt, and nutmeg. Stir frequently while cooking for about 15-20 minutes on medium heat. Allow to cool completely, then refrigerate for at least 60 minutes.

With your hands: shape the refrigerated Kroketten to ¾ the size of hotdogs, but a little thicker. (If they are too big they'll have to be deep fried for much longer.)

To Prepare the Crust
In three bowls: Bowl 1: add the flour. Bowl 2: add lightly beaten eggs. Bowl 3: add breadcrumbs. Drop the Kroketten into the first bowl. Roll and completely cover the Kroketten with flour, then dip into the eggs, then coat with the breadcrumbs. Be sure they are covered very well to create a "solid crust."

To Prepare the Kroketten
In a deep fryer: Heat the oil and fry the Kroketten until deep brown (or rich golden brown) for about 3-5 minutes.

Drain on paper towels. Serve with mustard as a dip.

*Ground chicken can be used as a substitute.

OLIE BALLEN
(Oil balls)

1 packet (7g) yeast
¼ cup water
2¼ cups flour (sifted)
2 teaspoons salt
1 cup milk
1 egg
1½ cups currants
¼ cup water (warm)
2 tablespoon anise
1 apple (peeled and minced)
3 cups cooking oil (for frying)
Powdered sugar (for dusting)

In a large cup: Dissolve 1 packet of yeast in ¼ cup water and let it stand for 10 minutes. In a large bowl: Mix together sifted flour and salt then add milk. Mix well. Add yeast mixture, egg, currants, anise, and apple. Cover the batter with a cloth and allow it to rise (at room temperature) to about twice its size.

In a deep fryer: Use two tablespoons to shape the batter into balls and drop them, one at a time, into the oil which should completely cover the balls. Fry until medium to dark brown (3-5 minutes).
Drain the balls on paper towels to remove any excess oil.
Sprinkle powdered sugar over oil balls while still warm.

Serve warm.

PASTECHIS
(Patties)

For the Filling
4 cooked chicken breasts (minced)*
¼ cup lemon juice
1 teaspoon black pepper
1 teaspoon paprika
½ cup currants
½ onion (minced)
1 sweet pepper (chopped)
1 garlic clove (minced)

For the Dough
1½ tablespoons margarine
2 eggs
¾ cup milk
3 cups flour (sifted)
1 tablespoon sugar
1 teaspoon salt
3 cups cooking oil (for frying)
1½ tablespoons olive oil

To Prepare the Filling
In a medium bowl: Cover minced chicken breasts with lemon juice. Add black pepper and paprika. Place in a sealed container and let marinate overnight in the refrigerator.
In a baking pan: Add chicken, currants, onion, sweet pepper, garlic, and olive oil. Mix well.

To Prepare the Dough
In a large bowl: Mix margarine, eggs and milk together. Slowly add flour with sugar and salt. Knead dough, and then roll out into a thin sheet. Cut dough into 8-inch circles.

To Prepare the Pastechis
Fill each circle with 3 tablespoons of chicken filling and fold the dough over so the edges meet. Use a fork to seal the edges.
In a deep fryer: Fry the sealed dough pouches until golden brown (3-5 minutes).
Drain excess oil on paper towels before serving.

*You can substitute ground beef or cheese (especially Dutch Gouda cheese) in place of the chicken.

PEAS SOUP

For the Soup
- ¾ cup red beans
- 1 tablespoon olive oil
- 2½ cups water
- 1 sweet potato
- ¼ of a pumpkin
- 3 tablespoons brown sugar
- 1 cup milk
- 1 celery stalk

For the Dumplings
- 1 tablespoon sugar
- 5 tablespoons butter
- 1 tablespoon cinnamon
- 3 tablespoons anise
- 1 egg
- ¼ cup milk
- 1 cup flour
- ¼ onion

To Prepare the Soup

In a medium bowl: Soak beans overnight (covered).

In a large deep sauce pan: Add beans with olive oil and cook in water for about 30-45 minutes on low-medium heat. Peel and cut sweet potato, and pumpkin into small to medium cubes, add to the cooking beans. Cook on low heat until pumpkin and sweet potato are medium tender, then add dumplings (see below), sugar, and milk. Cut celery and onion in small pieces and add to the sauce pan. Cook for about 20 minutes, occasionally stirring.

To Prepare the Dumplings

In a medium bowl: Combine sugar, butter, cinnamon, anise, egg, milk and flour. Mix well. Knead the dough, then roll into meatball-sized balls and add to the soup for the last 20 minutes of cooking time

PICA
(Hot onions)

2 large onions (minced)
3 jalapeno peppers
$^1/_8$ cup vinegar
1½ cups water

In a medium container: Add onions. Cut the peppers in three pieces and add, then pour in the vinegar and water. Cover and refrigerate overnight.

Pica can be stored in the refrigerator for up to a week.

Use Pica on fries with or without peanut sauce, on meats, poultry and fish.

Only serve the onions not the jalapeno peppers!

PINDA SAUCE
(Peanut sauce)

6 tablespoons peanut butter
1 teaspoon vegetable oil
1 cup water
1 teaspoon sugar
1 teaspoon salt
2 teaspoons soy sauce
Optional - 1 jalapeno pepper

In a small sauce pan over medium heat: Add peanut butter, oil and water; stir until the peanut butter has dissolved. Add sugar, salt and soy sauce. Continue to stir until mixture comes to a medium-thick consistency.

Optional: Cut pepper in about four pieces, then add to the pan for about 2-3 minutes; remove peppers before serving.

Use Peanut Sauce on potato fries, rice, or kabobs.

PRUNE CUPS

6 cups prunes
3 cups water
2 tablespoons oil
¾ cups brown sugar
5 tablespoons essence (either almond or rum)
½ tablespoon cinnamon
12 pre-made pie cups (or tart shells)

In a medium sauce pan: Cut prunes in 2-4 pieces each and cook in water, oil, and sugar, on medium heat (uncovered) for about 30 minutes. Stir frequently. Prunes will be done when they are very tender. Mix in essence and cinnamon.

Allow to cool for about an hour.

On a baking sheet: Space pie cups evenly on the sheet. Scoop 2-3 large tablespoons of the prune mixture into each pie cup. Refrigerate and serve cold.

RYSTEBRY

4 cups milk
2 vanilla pods (split open)
¾ cup pudding rice
6 tablespoons butter {dual usage}
4 tablespoons soft brown sugar {dual usage}
1 teaspoon cinnamon

In a large saucepan: Add milk and vanilla pods. Bring to a boil. Stir in rice, butter {5 tablespoons} and sugar {3 tablespoons} and return to a boil, stirring frequently. Lower heat and cook for 45-55 minutes and continue to stir.

Remove the vanilla pods before serving.

To serve: Add butter {1tablespoon} and sprinkle the cinnamon and remaining sugar {1 tablespoon} over the Rystebry.

SATE

For the Meat
1½ cups water
1 pound beef (stew)
1 tablespoon brown sugar
4 tablespoons Ketjap Manis*
Salt and pepper to taste
3-4 tablespoons vegetable oil (for frying)

For the Peanut Sauce
4 tablespoons peanut butter
¾ cup water
½ teaspoon Ketjap Manis*
1 tablespoon brown sugar
½ onion (minced)

To Prepare the Meat
In a large sauce pan: Add water, meat, sugar, Ketjap Manis, salt, and pepper, and cook for about an hour on low heat.

In a frying pan: Add meat and fry lightly for about 7-8 minutes over medium heat. Set aside.

To Prepare the Peanut Sauce
In a small sauce pan: Add peanut butter and water. Mix until peanut butter melts over low to medium heat. Then add Ketjap Manis, sugar, and onion. Stir gently until moderately thick. (Be careful not to overcook, it should not harden.)

To Prepare the Sate
Skewer the meat. The peanut sauce can be poured over the skewered meat or the peanut sauce can be used as a dip.

*Traditional Ketjap Manis is available at Dutchsweets.com

STOBA
(Sweet stew)

3 pounds beef stew meat
5 tablespoons black pepper
4 cups water {dual usage}
2 sweet potatoes
1 tablespoon olive oil

1 cup mixed vegetables*
1 jalapeno pepper
½ onion
¼ cup barbecue sauce

In a medium baking pan: Season beef with black pepper then cover and refrigerate overnight.

Add water {2 cups} and bake for 1 hour, covered, at 350°.

In a small sauce pan (or microwave-safe bowl): Peel and cut sweet potatoes into medium cubes. Cook sweet potatoes to medium softness. Do not overcook!

In a large sauce pan: Add water {2 cups}, olive oil and mixed vegetables, cook for about 10 minutes. Cut jalapeno in half, cut onion in medium cubes and add along with the barbecue sauce. Cover and cook for about 10 minutes.

Finally, add the beef to the sauce pan and allow it to simmer, on low heat, for about 30 minutes, covered. Add the sweet potatoes during the final 15 minutes. Stir frequently and remove the jalapeno peppers before serving.

Serve with rice.

*Frozen mixed vegetables work well in this recipe

STOOFPEREN
(Stewed pears)

8 pears (almost ripened)
1 bottle of red wine
3 cloves of garlic (minced)
1 tablespoon cinnamon
1 tablespoon dark brown sugar
½ teaspoon grated orange rind
½ teaspoon grated lemon rind
¼ teaspoon nutmeg
1 tablespoon olive oil

In a large saucepan: Peel the pears, leaving stems intact. Cut a thin slice from the bottom of each pear so that they will stand upright. Pour in the wine to cover the tops of the pears. Add cinnamon, sugar, rinds (lemon, orange), nutmeg, and oil. Bring to a boil, and then reduce heat to simmer for about 30 minutes.

Serve as a dessert or side dish.

STUFFING

1½ pounds chicken gizzards (minced)
¼ cup lemon juice
2 tablespoons brown sugar
½ teaspoon black pepper
½ onion (minced)
½ red, green, yellow pepper (minced)
3 garlic cloves (minced)
1 celery stalk (minced)
1 tablespoon soy sauce
½ cup currants
2 packs of crackers (crushed)*
1 cup water
2 tablespoons cooking oil (for frying)

In a large frying pan: Rinse gizzards with lemon juice and fry on low heat (2 tablespoons of oil) for about 3-4 minutes. Add sugar, black pepper, onion, peppers, garlic and celery. Continue to fry for about 2 minutes, adding oil if needed. Finally, add soy sauce, currants, and crackers,* and water; mix well until softened.

*Pour crackers into a bowl or kitchen towel and crush as finely as possible.

Stuffing can be added to your whole chicken before or after baking.

Made in the USA
Lexington, KY
15 February 2015